Gabriella Garofano Cannella
Nana Surameli

Traditional
Georgian
cuisine

- cookbook -

ALBERO NIRO
·EDITORE·

TRADITIONAL GEORGIAN CUISINE
Gabriella Garofano Cannella
Nana Surameli

Curated by: Alessandra Borroni
Editorial project: Albero Niro Editore
Illustration: Alessandra Borroni
info@alberoniro.it
Copyright © 2021 Alessandra Borroni

ISBN: 9798742677321
Independently published

Index

Presentation

During my first trip to Russia I went to a Georgian restaurant, I had never been there. When I started reading the menu, my gaze wandered in search of a known word but it kept scrolling strange names of dishes that for a Western were difficult to decipher. So, with the help of the waiter, who spoke only Russian, and almost randomly I chose "Khinkali" and "Adjarian Khachapuri".

The arrival of the dishes was a feast for my eyes and the first bite was a treat for my palate. The forms of food were extravagant, inviting but almost unknown. The most beautiful surprise was the goodness of those dishes.

When I came back in Italy I realized that Georgian cuisine, so famous in the great Russian land (spread by Joseph Stalin himself that we all know), was completely unknown in my country. I looked for some Georgian restaurants even in big cities... but nothing! The only way to eat Georgian dishes was to cook them, so I started my experimentation.

A few years later I decided to visit Georgia and here I had the opportunity to deepen the great gastronomic culture of this country, not only by tasting the dishes but also participating in cooking classes. The idea of creating a book to spread Georgian cuisine was born here.

At my side in the drafting of recipes there was Nana, a very good Georgian cook, who guided me step by step in the realization of the dishes and in the adaptation of the ingredients and procedures so as to succeed in preserving the original flavors with Western products.

Have a good trip through Georgian delights!

Presentation

Eating in Georgia

In a country where the word "friend" (*megobari*) literally means "the one who eats from the same plate", and in which the guest is always considered a gift, it is easy to understand that conviviality and good food are two fundamental elements of its culture. Georgian cuisine fully reflects this premise, its dishes are the reflection of hospitality, abundance, honesty, vivacity in colors and flavors.

Georgian banquets are famous all over the world, they take their name from the tablecloth of the laid table, in georgian language "*supra*".

There are two types of banquet *keipi* (festive supra) and *kelekhi* (dark supra). The first is a joyful banquet, and the second is a banquet that is held after the funeral.

The supra is always accompanied by good Georgian wine and the same banquet takes place through consecutive toasts guided by a "*tamada*". Tamada is the person in charge of leading the table dictating the rhythm of drinking. He must be a person with great oratory skills because toasts are not accompanied by a few words but by real speeches, often philosophical or spiritual, touching themes such as love, friendship, life etc. The *tamanda* must certainly be able to drink large amounts of wine without showing signs of drunkenness...

When you come to a banquet cold dishes are already on the well-laid out table. For example we can find fried eggplants stuffed with nuts (*nigvzians badrijani*), vegetable meatballs and nuts (*pkhali*), classic Georgian salad (*salati nigzvit)*, offal with pomegranate (*kuchmachi*), bread (*puri*), pickles, sauces etc. and this is just the beginning. After the cold dishes will begin to arrive by hand hot dishes such as grilled meat (*mtsvadi*) in various forms served with sauces, soups and stews (*chakapuli*), bread with melted cheese (*khachapuri*), juicy dumplings (*khinkali*) and so on, the amount of dishes is usually endless, until you get to sweets.

Fresh vegetables are a key part of Georgian cuisine: eggplant, tomatoes, onions, peppers, spinach, mushrooms. These are accompanied by pork, veal, chicken and turkey, various cheeses (including *sulguni*), eggs and fish.

Even the bakery (with all its tasty variations) here is an art.

Among all the ingredients in my opinion the nuts encloses the soul to Georgian cuisine and gives it a typical connotation. They are used for the preparation of most dishes, vegetables, meat, cheese and, of course, are widely used for the preparation of sweets.

In 2017 the Georgian Supra was included in the list of intangible cultural heritage of Georgia by UNESCO.

So let's have a toast in Georgia and start our journey... *"Gaumarjos"*!

Regional cuisine

Georgia is a small country but it contains in itself a vast culinary tradition dictated by the various regions of its territory.

In the kitchen of **Abkhazeti** the distinctive dish is roast chicken with *ajika* sauce. For the rest many nuts are used, for example in *apyrpylchapa* (stewed peppers), in *aritsvmgeli* (bread), in *akutaghchapa* (stuffed eggs). Another typical dish is *abkhazura* (spicy fried meatballs).

The cuisine of the **Adjara** region offers a wide variety of dishes, probably because it is a region exposed to influences determined by different factors, the sea, the mountains and a great history. The best known dish however is *adjaruli khachapuri* the famous bread stuffed with cheese, also *achma* is a typical dish, it is a kind of lasagna with cheese, it is considered another type of *khachapuri*.

In the **Guria** region *satsivi* (dishes with chicken meat) are very popular, *badrijani nigvzit* (eggplant rolls stuffed with nuts) are also very popular like *mchadi* (corn bread) and *kupati* (pork sausages). The most peculiar dish is the delicious *khachapuri* of the region that is baked in the period of Orthodox Christmas, it is in the shape of a half moon and stuffed with cheese and boiled eggs.

The cuisine of **Imereti** has many affinities with that of Guria, it is distinguished by the popular *imeruli khachapuri* (bread stuffed with cheese, eggs and butter), *pkhali* (walnut meatballs and herbs such as spinach and cabbage), the *kuchmachi* (chicken offal with walnut sauce and pomegranate juice) and for its cheeses.

The **Kakheti** is famous for its wines (Alazani, Akhasheni, Saperavi, and Kindzmarauli). It is home to the typical sweet *churchkhela* (dessert of nuts and grape juice). Meat dishes such as *mtsvadi* (pieces of meat coocked on skewer), or meat soups such as *chakapuli, chikhirtma, chanakhi* are most appreciated.

Cartalia is a region rich in delicious fruits such as peaches, apples and vegetables. Its cuisine is rich in soups and many vegetarian dishes. A typical appetizer is *jonjoli*, the shoots of a local plant preserved pickled.

In **Ossetia** *khachapuri* is stuffed with cheese and potatoes, it is called *khabizgina*.

Mingrelia is home to the most used cheese the *sulguni*, characterized by cow's milk spun pasta, it is often compared to mozzarella. The cuisine of this region is the most famous in Georgia, it is distinguished by many spices and nuts. Here are born dishes such as *elarji* (corn porridge with melted cheese), *mingrelian khachapuri* (bread stuffed with melted cheese), *ajika* (sauce of peppers and spices).

The mountain regions **Mtianeti, Khevi, Khevsureti, Pshavi** and **Tusheti** are famous for beer, which is perfect for accompanying *khinkali* (dumplings stuffed with meat or potatoes or cheese). The typical *guda* cheese of sheep's milk is produced in **Tusheti**.

Racha and **Lekhchumi** share many similar dishes such as *shkmeruli* (fried chicken seasoned with garlic sauce), *lobio* (bean soup), *lobiani* (khachapuri stuffed with bean paste).

Samtskhe and **Javakheti** are two regions that offer a little different cuisine, in part because the regions have Turkish origins, but also because here the people makes extensive use of goose meat. Here you can find dishes such as *batis shechamandi* (goose soup), *meskhuri khinkali* (dumplings of goose meat) *apokht* (dried meat of goose or duck), or dishes with ground snails. A particular dish is *tatarberak* pieces of boiled pasta seasoned with a sauce of melted butter, fried onion and yogurt *matsoni*. These regions are famous for dried fruits (*chiri*).

Finally the **Svaneti** region, nestled in the mountains of the Caucasus, is famous for its traditional dishes. *Kubdari* is the typical khachapuri stuffed with pork, the original version is made with cut and unminced meat. *P'et-vraal* is another kind of khachapuri stuffed with cheese and millet; *chvishtar* is a corn bread stuffed with cheese. The typical soup is *kharshil* (a soup made with barley and nettle. Svaneti is also famous for its spicy salt.

HERBS AND SPICES

Khmeli Suneli

- mixture of Georgian spices -

In Georgian recipes we will often find a strange ingredient called *Khmeli Suneli*, in Georgian language these words simply mean "dried herbs". There are many versions of this mix of spices and each family has its own personal.

This balanced mix of herbs reflects the position that Georgia occupies geographically, between Europe and the East. *Khmeli Suneli* is reminiscent of Indian curry with the freshness of European herbs, in this mix turmeric is replaced by the sweet Georgian "saffron", that is the powder of marigold petals (*zaprana*).

The most important herbs, which will rarely miss in this mix are blue fenugreek (*utskho suneli*) and coriander (*kindzi*); often we will also find savory (*kondari*) and Roman mint (*ombalo*).

All herbs are dried and reduced to powder with mortar or coffee grinder. They can be stored for a few months in a cool, dry place.

These are some of the endless possible recipes:

Recipe n°1

* 2 tsp
 of blue fenugreek seeds
* 2 dried laurel leaves
* 1 tbs ground coriander
* 1 tbs savory
* 1 and 1/2 tsp dried dill
* 1/2 tsp pepper

Recipe n°3

* 2 tbsp
 of ground coriander seeds
* 1 tbsp blue fenugreek
* 1 tbsp sweet paprika
* 2 tbsp of marigold petals

Recipe n°2

* 2 tsp ground coriander
* 2 tsp dried basil
* 2 tsp dill
* 2 tsp savory
* 1 tsp parsley
* 1 tsp mint
* 1 tsp blue fenugreek
* 1 tsp of marigold petals
* 1 bay leaf

SAUCES
Satsebela

Bazhe

- walnut sauce -

Bazhe is a Georgian sauce made from nuts, it is often used to accompany meat, fish and vegetables, or as a basis for more complex dishes.
For Georgian people the cuisine sauces have great importance. They serve sauces to enrich the taste of food but also to introduce vitamins, bioactive components, antioxidants and to promote the process of assimilation of food.

SLURP!

Ingredients:

* 5 oz of walnuts
* 1 or 2 teeth of garlic
* 1 ¾ cup of water
* 1 tbsp of blue fenugreek
* ½ puppy of marigold in powder (or saffron)
* ½ tsp paprika
* Pepper
* Sale
* 2 tsp vinegar or juice
* Lemon (optional)

Crush the nuts in a mortar (or food grinder) and set aside the oil they will produce. Finely chop the garlic and then grind it with mortar and pestle add nuts and spices, stirring well. Add the necessary water and or mix until the cream is soft and homogeneous. If it is to your taste you can add a few drops of lemon or vinegar.

Tkemali
- plum sauce -

Tkemali is the Georgian name of a variety of wild plums, as well as a famous sauce prepared from the plums themselves. This sauce has an important place in Georgian cuisine, to make a comparison tkemali sauce is for Georgians similar to ketchup for Americans. The sauce is used as a dressing for fried, grilled dishes, poultry and potatoes. Green tkemali sauce is prepared in spring with unripe plums, instead the red tkemali sauce is made towards the end of summer with ripe plums.

Ingredients:

* 2,2 lb plums
* 5 teeth of garlic
* 1 ½ level tbsp of salt
* A pinch of dill
* A pinch of roman mint
* 2 tsp coriander
* 2 tsp salt
* Little chili
* Add 1 or 2 tsp of sugar if the plums are particularly sour.

Wash the plums and put them in a deep saucepan. Add a cup of water and bring it to a boil. Lower the temperature and continue cooking over low heat for 10-15 minutes until the plums are soft. Drain the plums and place them in a bowl, separately store the cooking water. Cut the plums in half and remove the core. Put a sieve on a bowl and add the plums with a little bit of cooking water to soften them. Squeeze them with force to bring out the pulp. With a mincer chop the peeled garlic with all the herbs, spices and salt. Now combine the mixture to the plum pulp and mix thoroughly with a wooden spoon. Add a little bit of cooking water until the sauce is creamy and homogeneous. Cook over low heat for 40 minutes.

Allow the sauce to cool and store it in the refrigerator.

You can also store it in airtight sterilized glass jars and boiled in a water bath.

Tkemali sauce can be served with meat dishes, poultry and potatoes.

Adjika
- pepper sauce -

Adjika is a spicy sauce whose main ingredient is chili pepper. The original recipe comes from Abkhazia, a Caucasian state claimed by Georgia, but in fact independent. Here the ancient recipe is made with dried chillies, garlic and spices mashed with a stone and reduced to paste. We offer a slightly softer version suitable for the western taste, in which tomatoes and sweet peppers are also introduced. It is used especially in winter to accompany meat and vegetables.

Ingredients:

* 1 lb sweet peppers (paprika)
* 7 oz tomatoes
* 2 oz red chillies
* 8 teeth of garlic
* 2 tbsp of blue fenugreek powder
* 1 tbsp of coriander powder
* Oil
* 1 tbsp of apple cider vinegar
* Salt

Clean the sweet peppers and chillies removing all the seeds, pass them in a vegetable grinder and cook for about 15/20 minutes so that the mince softens lose water and reduce. Meanwhile, peel the tomatoes and squeeze them, clean the garlic teeth and chop everything, add the spices, oil, vinegar and a little salt, then pour them into the saucepan. Continue cooking for about 15/20 minutes to stir and thicken the sauce. Can be stored in glass jars.

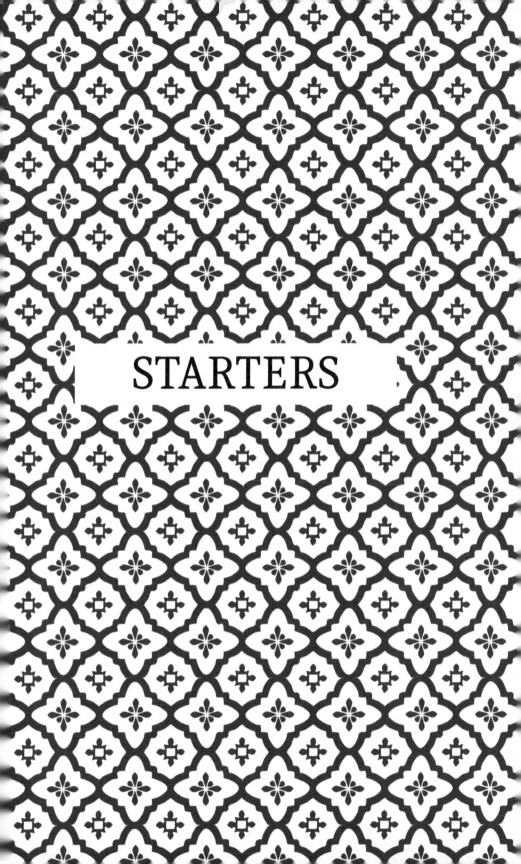

STARTERS

Pkhali
- spinach and walnut balls -

Pkhali are vegetable meatballs typical of Georgian cuisine. They can be composed of mixed vegetables such as cabbage, eggplant, beans, beets, spinach or from a single vegetable. My favorites are those made with spinach.

Ingredients:

* 1 lb of fresh spinach
* 2 cloves of garlic
* 1 cup walnut kernels
* Half onion
* Milled marigold or saffron
* Coriander
* Blue Fenugreek
* Paprika
* Vinegar or lemon juice
* Salt
* Pepper
* Pomegranate seeds

Wash and dry the spinach then put them to cook in boiling salted water for 5 minutes. Drain and immediately throw them in a bowl with cold water. Drain well once again and finely cut the cooked leaves. Chop and mix all the other ingredients: nuts, onion, garlic, marigold, coriander, paprika, fenugreek, a little bit of vinegar, salt and pepper. Add the mixture to the spinach and make balls with your hands. Usually they are decorated with pomegranate seeds.

Badrijani
- fried eggplants stuffed with nuts -

Badrijani or more precisely *Niguzit Badrijani* are tasty eggplant rolls filled with walnut sauce. They are part of the Georgian appetizers, best served cold.

Ingredients:

* 2,2 lb of long eggplant
* 1 ½ cups of shelled walnuts
* ¼ coast of celery
* ½ tsp of khmeli suneli, you can replace it with spices to your taste
* 2 cloves of garlic
* Vegetable oil
* Onion (optional)
* ½ or 1 glasses of water
* Vinegar
* Salt
* Pomegranate seeds

Cut the eggplant in length by making slices about 5-7 mm of thickness. Put them in salt for about 1-2 hours, then drain and dry. Fry them in vegetable oil. Drain well from excess oil.

To prepare the sauce finely chop the nuts with garlic, onion, spices and salt. Little at a time add hot water to the mince so as not to exceed, stir until a homogeneous and rather thick sauce is obtained.

Maximum two hours before serving spread the sauce obtained on the slices of eggplant then rolled the slices creating rolls. Garnish with pomegranate seeds and lettuce leaves.

Ajapsandali
- Eggplant stew -

Ajapsadali is a popular dish of the Transcaucasian regions: Georgia, Armenia and Azerbaijan. It is usually consumed in summer when the land offers a great wealth of fresh vegetables. There are many versions with different vegetables, and each family has its own recipe, however the main ingredient always remains eggplant. The dish is served cold after a rest of at least 4 hours or better overnight.

Ingredients:

* 1 lb eggplant
* 1 lb tomato
* 1 large potato
* 1 onion
* 1 bell pepper
* 2 tbsp oil
* 2 teeth of garlic
* Parsley, coriander, dill
* Sale
* Pepper
* Chili pepper (optional)

Bake the eggplant in the oven at 375°F (190°C) for 35/40 minutes. While cooking, boil the potatoes and then cut into cubes. Blanch the tomatoes for 10 minutes then squeeze them and mash the pulp with a fork. Stew the onions in oil and add the tomato sauce with the chopped pepper and garlic. Cook on low heat for about ten minutes. Peel the eggplant, cut them into small pieces and add them to the tomato together with the pieces of boiled potatoes. Add all the herbs and spices, season with salt and pepper and simmer for another 5 minutes.

Let cool before serving.

Soko ketze

- mushrooms filled with cheese -

A very simple but at the same time tasty dish are the mushrooms filled cheese or *Soko Ketze*. Frequently we can find them among the menu of appetizers. Mushrooms are cooked and served in a clay bowl.

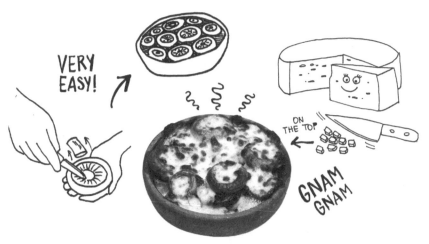

VERY EASY!

ON THE TOP

GNAM GNAM

Photo by courtesy of *Tabla Saloon Restaurant* - Tbilisi

Ingredients for 3 servings:

* 1 lb of champignon mushrooms
* 6 oz butter
* 4 oz Sulguni cheese (or mozzarella and feta mix)

Cut the cheese into small pieces. Clean the mushrooms and carefully remove the stems leaving only the heads. Grease the clay bowls and insert the mushrooms inside with the heads turned over, so that the hollow part remains on top. Add a small piece of butter inside each mushroom and put the remaining in the bowls.

Bake in the oven and cook at 350°F (180°C) for 20 minutes. Then add the cheese to each mushroom and cook on low heat for another 20 minutes.

Serve them hot with a sprinkling of black pepper.

Mchadi
- Corn bread -

Mchadi is a popular Georgian corn bread. Each region has its own version of mchadi but it is usually served hot and accompanied by cheeses and *lobio* (bean paste).

Photo *Georgia About* - Creative Commons

Ingredients:

* 3 cups of corn flour
* 1 ½ cups approx. of water
  (depends on flour)
* A pinch of salt
* Seed oil

Pour corn flour and salt into a bowl.

Begin to knead gradually pouring water and making sure that the dough is firm and not wet.

Make balls and flatten them creating an oblong shape of about 7-10 cm.

In a frying pan heat the oil to medium temperature, when the oil is ready put the "pancakes" and cover with a lid for 5-6 minutes. Flip them over and cook them on the other side too. Serve them hot.

Kuchmachi

- offal with pomegranate -

Kuchmachi is a traditional dish of Georgian cuisine consisting of offal. They can be pork, beef or chicken. Some regions add walnut sauce.

Photo by courtesy of Megruli Sakhli Restaurant - Tbilisi

Ingredients:

* 1 lb offal (liver, heart and tongue of beef or chicken or pork)
* 2 garlic cloves crushed to the mortar
* ½ onion
* 1 pomegranate
* Blue fenugreek
* Marigold powder or saffron
* Dried coriander
* ½ tsp vinegar
* Pepper
* Salt

Put the meat to boil with water, garlic and bay leaf in a saucepan with lid. Cook it on low heat for about 2 hours, remove the foam that it will form. When the meat is cooked, drain it and let it cool. Cut the offal into small cubes. Add salt, pepper, spices and crushed garlic. Finely chop the onion and add it to the meat with vinegar. Finally add the pomegranate seeds and mix everything.

It should be served cold.

Elardzhi

- polenta with cheese -

Elardzhi is a tasty polenta to be served hot. It consists of corn and spun paste cheese. The original corn used for this polenta is white, not because it is born white but because it undergoes a particular bleaching process... We can also use traditional corn flour.

Photo by courtesy of *Megruli Sakhli Restaurant* - Tbilisi

Ingredients:

* 3 cups corn flour for polenta
* 5 cups of water
* 1,7 lb sulguni cheese
(or mix of mozzarella and feta)

Pour the water into a pot (possibly copper or cast iron), put it on the fire and bring it to a boil. Meanwhile, cut the cheese into thin slices. When the water boils gradually pour the flour stirring with a wooden spoon until the polenta begins to thicken. Lower the heat and add the cheese continuing to stir until the corn is cooked.

When the mixture becomes uniform and spun turn off the heat and spread the polenta on the plates with a wet wooden spoon.

It should be served very hot.

Khinkali

- dumplings -

Khinkali is one of the most well-known dishes of Georgian cuisine. This strange name hides delicious dumplings. Usually they are stuffed with meat but also the variant with cheese or mushrooms is delicious.

The many folds of the dough of which the dumplings are formed are their main feature, they seem to form an inverted chef's hat.

In Georgia doing these folds is considered an art: the more the better!

In ancient times the *khinkali* were made in honor of the goddess of the sun Barbale (became with Christianity Santa Barbara), the folds represent the rays of the sun, the true tradition in fact provides 28 folds that represent the 28 years of the solar cycle.

Ingredients:

* 1 lb pork and beef
* 1 or 2 onions
* 2 cups of flour
* 1 small cup of water
* Coriander or parsley
* Paprika
* Cumin (optional)
* Pepper
* Salt

Chop together meat and onions. Add the coriander, your favorite spices, pepper, salt and a little hot water so that the filling is not dry.

For the dough put the flour in a bowl and make a hole in the middle, pour warm water and salt into it. Knead until the mixture is uniform and not too soft.

Put the dough in an airtight container (or cover with cling film) and let it stand in the refrigerator for 40 minutes. Take the dough back and divide it into 25 equal pieces. For each piece form a ball. Roll out the dough balls thinly in circular shape until you reach a diameter of about 15cm.

Put a tablespoon of minced meat in each circle. Take one side and start making folds clockwise, shaping them like a fis. The more folds there are the better! Cut the dough of the excess stem.

Boil the water with salt, when boiling gently pour the *khinkali* so that they do not touch each other. From time to time gently stir to prevent them from sticking. After about 7-8 minutes they will be cooked, you will know because when the *khinkali* come to the surface they will be ready. Drain and place them in a plate.

They must be served with a sprinkling of black pepper and accompanied with a good beer!

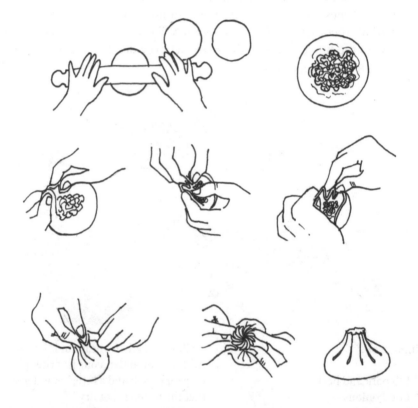

The khinkali should be eaten strictly with the hands. Hold it for the stem. Care not to leak out the internal juice that should be drunk immediately after the first bite. The petiole should not be eaten, it is only used to hold the dumpling and to dip it in tasty Georgian sauces.

Khinkali Qvelit
- dumplings with cheese and mint -

Khinkali Qvelit is the vegetarian variant, usually it is filled with cheese and mint. It is more delicate and just as tasty!

Ingredients for 25 khinkali:

* 2 cups of flour
* 1 small cup of water
* 1 tsp salt
* 25 oz suluguni cheese
 (or mix of mozzarella and feta)
* ½ cup of sour cream
* 3 beaten eggs
* Finely chopped mint
* Coriander or parsley
* Ground black pepper

In a bowl mix the flour together with salt and warm water, knead until a smooth ball is formed. Put the dough in an airtight container or cover with cling film and let it stand in the refrigerator for 40 minutes. Meanwhile in a bowl mix the cheese, sour cream, mint, coriander, eggs, salt and pepper.

Take the dough back and divide it into 25 equal pieces. For each piece form a ball. Roll out the dough in a circular form until it reaches a diameter of about 15cm.

Place 1 or 2 tbsp of the cheese mixture in the middle of each and close them by folding the edges over the filling, as described in the previous page.

When the *khinkali* are ready bring to a boil a large pot of salted water, pour the kinkhali and cook about 8 minutes, drain and serve hot, with ground black pepper.

Achma

- cheese lasagna -

Achma is a kind of cheese lasagna that is usually done in the regions of Adjara and Abkhazia. The crispy top crust contrasts with the tender inner layers of cheese. In Georgia, the choice of cheese is generally determined by local production, so feel free to experiment with any combination of cheese, but remember that it is better to avoid mixing too many different cheeses.

Photo credit © Adjara.Travel

Ingredients:

* 1 ⅓ cups of flour
* ½ tsp salt
* 3 eggs
* 4 cups of water
* 3 oz of liquid butter
* 7 oz of feta coarsely crumbled
* 7 oz of crumbled mozzarella

Knead the flour, eggs, milk and salt until the mixture is homogeneous. Form a ball, cover it with a cling film and let it stand for at least 30 minutes.

Roll out the dough as thin as possible then cut the pasta sheet obtained into large pieces like your baking pan. Grease the pan with the butter. Blanch the pasta sheets in salted water for 1 minute, then pass them in cold water and dry with paper towels.

Place the pasta sheet in the baking pan and spread a layer of butter on it.

Repeat the same procedure for the second sheet. On the third layer put the mixed cheeses.

Repeat the procedure for all the layers by putting butter on them. Usually in Georgia you make a single layer of cheese and in all the others you put butter but you can also alternate the layers.

Cut into portions and on top of the last layer of fresh pasta spread the liquid butter. Bake in a preheated oven at 390°F (200°C) for 30 minutes. Let cool for a couple of minutes and serve.

Blinchiki
S Myasom

- stuffed crepes with meat -

Blinchiki S Myasom are thin crepes filled with meat, the main feature is in the filling that must be quite juicy.

Ingredients:

* 7/8 cups of flour
* 2 cups of milk
* 2 eggs
* 2 tsp seed oils
* 1 tsp sugar
* 1 tsp baking soda
* 7 oz of minced lean veal
* Butter
* Onion
* Salt and pepper

In advance cook in a pan the minced meat with chopped onion, a little bit of butter, salt and pepper. Do not let it dry too much but let there be some juice. (If you prefer a more delicate flavor you can also boil it.)

Prepare the crepes now. Beat the eggs with the whisk then add the sugar, a pinch of salt and oil. Pour the milk continuously beating and add the sifted flour, baking soda. Beat until the dough is uniform.

Heat a lightly oiled pan, when it is hot pour a little batter into it. Turn the pan to enlarge the bater and cover the entire surface. When the first side is cooked flip the crepe and cook the second side.

As they are cooked, remove them from the heat and spread on them a thin layer of meat, roll them and close them well at the edges, so as not to leak the juice of the meat.

Again heat the pan slightly oiled. Cook the *blinchiki* on medium heat until they are golden brown on both sides. Serve them warm.

Tolma
- vine leaves rolls -

The tolma also called "dolma" is a traditional dish of Transcaucasian Asia mainly from Georgia, Armenia, Azerbaijan, Turkey and Iran. In the most common version tolma are meat and rice rolls wrapped in vine leaves, but variants can be many. Often they are accompanied with yogurt sauce.

Photo credit by *Lesya Dolyk*

Ingredients for approx. 35/40 rolls:

* 40 fresh vine leaves with stems removed (or stored in brine)

Stuffing:
* 25 oz of ground low-fat beef
* ⅔ cup grain white rice
* 2 chopped yellow onions
* 2 tbsp tomato puree
* ½ small cup of sunflower oil (or oil vegetable with a delicate taste)
* Chopped aromatic herbs
* Salt
* Black pepper

Sauce:
* 1 cup of whole milk yogurt
* 2 cloves of garlic
* Salt

Soak the grape leaves in boiling water for about 1 minute so that they soften, then pass them under cold water and drain well. Mix all the ingredients for the filling.

Cover the bottom of a pan with a few grape leaves. Above we will lay the rolls that we are about to create.

Fill the rest of the leaves in this way: spread a leaf on a flat surface with the matte side upwards. With a spoon pour a little meat near the end of the stem, fold the sides of the leaf to cover it, then roll up.

Put the rolls in the pan with the seam facing down. Cover them and press them with a plate.

Pour enough salted water until the *tolma* is covered. Bring to a boil and then lower the heat, cover and boil over low heat for 30-40 minutes, until the meat and rice are cooked.

While the rolls are cooking prepare the sauce by mixing the yogurt, garlic and salt together.

When the rolls are cooked, carefully remove them from the water using a spoon. Serve them hot with the yogurt sauce above.

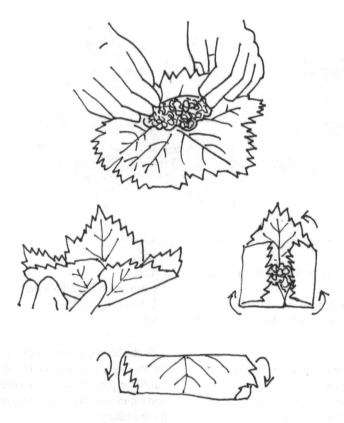

Closure of vine leaves

Salati Nigvzit
- Salad with walnut sauce -

Salati Niguzit is a fresh salad consisting of fresh summer vegetables with herbs, all seasoned with walnut sauce.

Ingredients:

* Tomatoes
* Green peppers
* Red onion
* Cucumbers
* Coriander or fresh parsley
* Purple basil
* Shelled walnuts
* Marigold dried powder
* Ground coriander
* Wine vinegar
* Salt
* Pepper

Using a mortar (or meat grinder) crush the nuts with a clove of garlic, a pinch of calendula powder, a pinch of ground cilantro and a pinch of salt. Add 1 teaspoon of wine vinegar, 1 teaspoon of water (or more, depending on taste) and mix.

Now cut fresh vegetables: tomatoes, cucumbers, peppers, onions and put them in a salad bowl. Add the walnut sauce and a drizzle of oil or vinegar and mix the salad well.

Spread with basil and chopped cilantro. The salad is ready!

BREAD
Puri

Shotis Puri

- bread -

In Georgia bread is served with every dish. *Puri* is a type of flat bread soft inside and crispy outside. It is baked in open circular ovens made of clay (called *tone*), we who do not have such an oven could bake it on a terracotta floor.

The following recipe also puts a little sugar that gives to the bread a beautiful amber color and makes sure that it keeps longer.

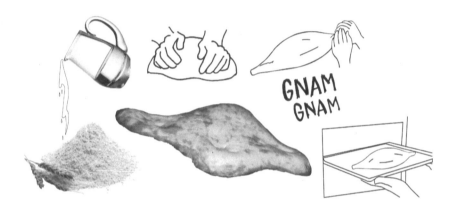

Dose for 3 loaves:

* 4 ½ cups of flour
* 3 cups of warm water
  (for a softer dough you can
  replace it in part with milk)
* 2 tsp of dry brewer's yeast
* 2 tbsp of salt
* 2 level tsp of sugar (optional)

Pour all the dry ingredients (flour, salt, sugar) on a board, then form a hole in them and pour warm water and yeast (previously dissolved in a little water).

Begin to mix the ingredients with your hands and knead the dough for 5 minutes. When it is homogeneous cover with a damp cloth (or with cling film) and let it rise for about 1 hour and a half or 2 hours, until doubling.

Now divide the dough into 3 equal parts and put them on a floured board, knead well and give an oblong shape, like a boat. Cover the loaf and let them stand again for 10 minutes.

Before baking, spread the shape with your hands making it thinner (about 1 cm thick), then put it on top of the hot oven at about 220°C.

In about 8/10 minutes the bread will bake and turn out to be golden.

To make it soft, spray the pure warm water and wrap it in a tea towel.

Khachapuri

Khachapuri is a rich leavened bread stuffed with butter and cheese, it can be considered the real Georgian national dish. For its goodness khachapuri is loved by everyone: Georgians and foreigners.

Each region has its own variant, usually made with local cheese. For example, *imeruli khachapuri* takes its name from the fresh cheese, made from cow's milk, produced in the Imereti region; the *megruli khachapuri*, from the Samegrelo region, differs because it adds a generous dose of cheese on the top; the *adjaruli khachapuri*, from the region of Adjara, has the typical boat shape and in the top in addition to the cheese has the egg and butter.

In the Racha region the typical *lobiani khachapuri* is filled with a bean paste. In Svaneti we find the *kubdari khachapuri* stuffed with pork cut into small pieces or the *p'etvraal khachapuri* stuffed with four different cheeses. In Ossetia the khachapuri is made with a filling of cheese and potatoes.

Penovani khachapuri is native to Samtskhe-Javakheti, has a square or triangular shape and is stuffed with a mix of Imeruli and Sulguni cheeses combined with egg yolks. In Guria the festive khachapuri is crescent shaped and has hard-boiled eggs.

IMERETIAN MEGRELIAN ADZHARIAN

LOBIANI SVANETIAN PENOVANI

KUBDARI

The dough recipe can be used as a basis for all variants of khachapuri.

Doses for 2 large khachapuri:

* 2 cups of flour
* 1 small cup of water (or kefir or milk)
* 1 egg (optional)
* 1 tbsp oil (sunflower or olive)
* 2 level tsp of dry brewer's yeast
  or 1 oz of fresh brewer's yeast
* 1 tsp of salt
* 1 tsp sugar

Dissolve the yeast in a little water, add the sugar and a tbsp of flour then let it stand for 15 minutes.

Put on the pastry board (or in a bowl) the remaining flour, salt and water (you can also add a little milk or kefir instead of water) the previously prepared yeast and oil. If you want to make the dough more full-bodied you can also add an egg.

Knead the ingredients well and after obtaining a soft and smooth mass put it to rise for about 2 hours, until the mass is doubled.

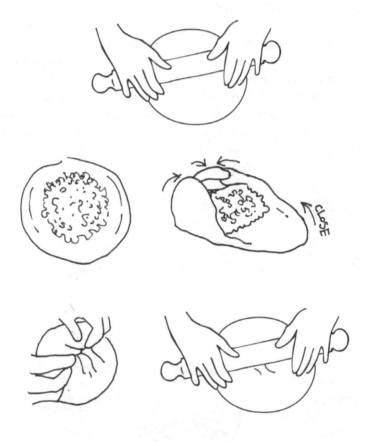

Imeruli Khachapuri

Imeruli Khachapuri
- cheese bread -

SERVE HOT!

Ingredients for 1 piece:

* 9 oz basic dough for khachapuri
* 3,5 oz of imereti cheese (or make a mix of mozzarella and feta)
* 1 egg
* Salt to taste
* 1 oz butter

Follow the basic recipe of the previously described khachapuri dough. While the dough rises, cut the cheese into small pieces, mix it with the egg and a little butter.

Roll out the dough in a circular way (how to make a pizza) and pour the cheese mixture in the center of it leaving the edge free.

Now take the outer edges of the circle as if it were a sack and close it on top. Roll out the dough again without letting out the cheese, when you have obtained the round shape make a pinch in the center breaking a bit of the surface dough (to prevent it swelling).

Spread the baking sheet with a little flour to prevent the khachapuri from sticking and place it inside.

Heat the oven to 356°F (180°C) and bake for about 15 minutes.

If you want to give a golden color to khachapuri 5 minutes before baking you can brush it with an egg yolk.

Freshly baked, pass butter on the surface, this will make it soft. It should be served well hot.

Adjarian Khachapuri

Adjarian Khachapuri

- bread with cheese and egg -

Ingredients for 1 khachapuri:

* 7 oz of dough for khachapuri
as per previous recipe.
* 5 oz sulguni cheese
(or mix of mozzarella and feta)
* 1 egg
* 0,5 oz butter

You can make the dough for khachapuri following the basic recipe on page 58. While the dough rises, prepare the stuffing. Cut the cheeses into small pieces and mix them together adding a little butter.

When the dough is leavened roll out the mass making an oval. Flour the baking tray a little and transfer the khachapuri onto it.

Put the cheese on top of the oval, and then roll the side edge, so that it is stuffed with cheese. Close the two ends to form a kind of boat. Cook at 180-200°C for 12-15 minutes.

When the khachapuri is cooked and the melted cheese open the oven and break an egg (or if you prefer only the yolk) over the cooked cheese. Let cook a few more minutes so that the yolk remains creamy. Take out the khachapuri from the oven and put on it a piece of butter.

The khachapuri is ready!

It should be eaten by breaking one of the ends with your hands and mixing with it the cheese and the egg.

Khachapuri Tarkhunit
- bread with cheese with fresh herbs -

Ingredients for 1 khachapuri:

* 7 oz of dough for khachapuri
* 7 oz cheese (mozzarella and feta)
* Fresh tarragon leaves
* Wild fennel
* Parsley
* 1 tsp salt
* 1 egg (optional)

In a large bowl, combine the crumbled cheeses, herbs and salt. Roll out the dough on a piece of lightly floured baking paper. Form a circle of 25cm in diameter and about 3mm thick. Spread half of the cheese mixture over the dough leaving a 5cm edge. On two opposite sides of the circle turn the edges leaving the cheese in the center. Close the narrower ends of the circle giving it a shape of a boat; put the other half of the cheese mixture in the middle.

Put the khachapuri in the baking tray and let rise for another 20 minutes.

Just before baking, lightly brush the edges with oil. Bake in a hot oven at 480°F (250°C) for about 16-18 minutes, until the cheese is melted and the dough is golden. Optionally a few minutes before baking you can break an egg over the stuffing. Serve it hot.

Merguli Khachapuri

- double cheese bread-

Ingredients for 1 khachapuri:

* 7 oz of dough for khachapuri
* 7 oz of cheese (mozzarella and feta)
* 1 egg
* A little piece of butter

In a large bowl combine the crumbled cheeses, beaten egg and butter.

Roll out the dough on a piece of lightly floured baking paper, form a circle of diameter 25cm and about 3mm thick.

Put more than half of the filling compound in the middle of the circle, then take the edges of the circle circumference and close the flaps as if it were a sack (see pag.58)

Carefully flatten the stuffed dough with the palm of your hand and fingers until it is round again.

Add the remaining cheese over the circle. If you want a golden color you can polish the outer edge with a beaten egg yolk.

Slightly sprinkle a baking tray with flour to prevent the khachapuri from sticking and place it in the hot oven preheated to 480°F (250°C) for about 15 minutes.

When it is cooked, remove it from the oven and rub the remaining 20g of butter on the surface.

Lobiani
- Bread with beans -

The *lobiani* is the typical meal of the Georgian festival of Barbaroba, the day of Santa Barbara (17 December) but in truth it is consumed all year round. In the region of Racha, region where the best lobiani is made, the beans are boiled together with their typical smoked ham. In our recipe we can replace it with bacon or smoked bacon but it is still an optional ingredient.

Ingredients (dose for 4 lobiani):

For pasta:

* 4 ½ cups of flour
* 2 tsp of dry yeast
* 1 egg
* 2 small cups of warm water
  or better kefir
* ½ tbsp of salt

For the filling:

* 1 lb red beans
* 11 oz ham or bacon
  or smoked bacon (optional)
* 3,5 oz butter,
* 4 or 5 bay leaves,
* 2 cloves of garlic (optional)
* salt.

Preparation of the filling.

Soak the beans overnight, this will sweeten them. Cut the bacon into small pieces and put it in a pot, fry for a few minutes together with garlic, add water, bay leaves, salt and boil for at least 1 hour. Meanwhile, prepare the dough.

Put in a bowl 4 cups of flour, 1 tsp of dry yeast, half a tsp of salt and 1 egg. Add the warm water and knead until a ball is formed. Cover the dough and leave in a warm place for at least 1 hour and a half to allow the dough to rise, it must double.

When the beans are cooked, remove them from the pot and put them in a bowl (remove ham, bay leaf, garlic) together with salt and 2/3 of butter (if you have not used the bacon in the previous step you will need to use 100 grams of butter). Crush the beans and butter well until they have the consistency of a mashed.

Take the yeast mass again, add 1/2 cup of flour and knead again until it's firm enough.

Flour a worktop and divide the dough into 4 balls. Flatten each ball with your hands to form a circular shape 1 cm thick.

Divide the lobiani mixture into 4 parts and place each part in the center of each of the 4 circles of dough.

Wrap the edges of the dough over the beans as if it were a bag then close it (see pag.52). Flatten with your hands the stuffed dough, taking care not to leak out the bean mix.

Use a knife to make small cuts and mark the wedges of the khachapuri.

Bake in the oven at 160-180°C for 15-20 minutes. An alternative is to bake the dough on a frying pan over medium-low heat for 7 minutes on each side. Traditional lobiani is rather pale.

When removing them from the oven rub the remaining butter on its surface and serve them hot.

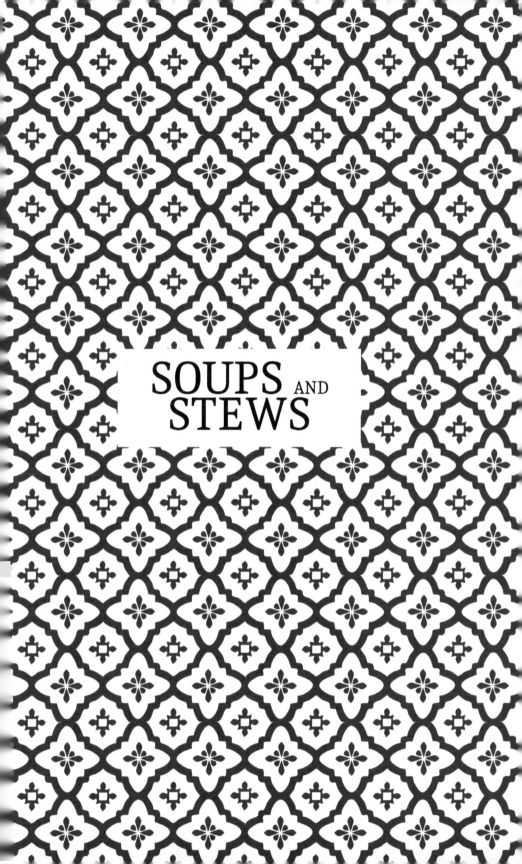

SOUPS AND STEWS

Lobio

- Bean soup -

Photo courtesy of *Tabla Saloon Restaurant* - Tbilisi

Ingredients:

* 1 lb of red beans
 (0,9 lb if they are dry)
* 3,5 oz onion
* 2 cloves of garlic
* A drizzle of oil
* Coriander
* Savory
* Mint
* Pepper
* Salt

If you want to use dried beans soak them in cold water at least 3 hours before cooking, or better still all night.

Pour the beans into a saucepan with salted water and bring them to a boil. When cooked, turn off the heat and leave them in the pot.

Put the chopped onion in a frying pan and brown it with a little oil. Pounded in a mortar garlic, mint, savory, pepper and a pinch of salt. Drain the beans, preserving the cooking water. Add them to the other ingredients and crush them coarsely with a wooden spoon.

Pour everything into a clay pot and add a cup of cooking water. Boil another 3-5 minutes over medium heat. Make portions in individual terracotta bowls and put in the oven before serving.

Matsvnis Supi
- Soup with yogurt -

Yogurt soup promotes good digestion and is very simple to do. Georgian yogurt, Matsuni, is slightly different from the European one, if you can get it you can remove sour cream from the ingredients listed below. This soup should not be heated, but it should be eaten right away.

Ingredients:

* 1 onion in small pieces
* 1 tbsp of olive oil (or sunflower)
* 4 cups whole yogurt
* ¼ cup sour cream
* 2 cups of water approx.
* 1 egg
* 2 cloves of garlic
* 1 tbsp flour
* A pinch of salt
* Chopped shallot
* Coriander or parsley

Heat the oil in a large saucepan. Add the onions and cook until they are completely soft. Meanwhile, mix the yogurt, water, egg, salt and garlic together with a blender. When the onions are soft add the yogurt mixture to the pot and bring it to a boil, stirring constantly. Let it boil slowly for about five minutes. If the soup seems too thick, add a little water to your preference. Season with salt and the soup will be ready. Garnish with chopped herbs and serve hot soup.

Chikhirtma
- soup of chicken broth and eggs-

The technique of *chikhirtma* soup originates in ancient Persia, its basis is made of chicken broth (or more rarely lamb). It is thickened with beaten eggs (or just yolks) and lemon curd. The inclusion of raw eggs in the hot broth is quite difficult.

Chicken broth is the basis of the recipe, we will describe below how to get it, but if you have it already ready you can skip this step.

Ingredients:

* 4 cups of chicken broth
* 5 eggs
* 2 medium-sized onions
* 3 tbsp flour
  (preferably corn)
* fresh cilantro or parsley
* 3 tbsp lemon
* Salt

The broth:

Put clean chicken (whole or in pieces) in a deep pot add 3 liters of water and bay leaves. Cook at a low temperature until the chicken is cooked, it will take about 2 and a half hours.

Remove the chicken and store the cooking broth that will serve for our dish. Chicken can be cut, salted and eaten together with broth or can be used to make a salad.

Soup:

In a frying pan stew over low heat finely chopped onions with the addition of a little water, they will have to be soft and white.

Sprinkle flour, salt, coriander and a little broth on them, mix well with a whisk. Then add all the filtered broth. Bring to a boil then cook over low heat until the end of the recipe.

Put 5 yolks in a bowl (if you want to use whole eggs 4) and whisk well, stirring with whisk add lemon juice and then add very slowly about 500 ml of chicken broth boiling always continuing to whisk.

Add everything to the pot with the broth and whisk constantly. Cook over low heat for a few minutes so that the eggs thicken slightly.

Adjust the salt, add a little mint and then remove the pot from the heat. Serve hot with a little fresh cilantro. You can put inside the dishes even a few pieces of boiled chicken.

Katmis Satsivi

- chicken with walnut sauce-

The tender chicken wrapped in creamy and aromatic walnut sauce is a traditional Georgian dish that will conquer your palate.

Ingredients:

* 2,2 lb of skinless chicken thighs
* 4 cups of chicken broth
* 3 cups of toasted walnut kernels
* 10 garlic cloves
* 1 large yellow onion
* ⅕ cup of olive oil
* 2 egg yolks
* 2 tbsp of red wine vinegar
* 3 tsp of paprika
* 1 tsp ground coriander
* 1 tsp ground fenugreek
* Chili pepper
* Coriander or parsley
* A pinch of cinnamon
* Salt and pepper

Put 3 cups of walnuts with a little broth in a food processor and reduce the mixture in a sauce. Add a little coriander, 5 garlic cloves, half an onion, a piece of chilli, salt and pepper. Blend until the mixture is smooth and homogeneous. Separately heat the oil in a saucepan over medium-high heat. Chop the chicken legs with salt and pepper, then put them to cook in the saucepan for about 8 minutes until golden brown, turn as needed. Add the remaining garlic and onions, continue cooking for a few more minutes, stirring occasionally, sprinkle with paprika, coriander, fenugreek and cinnamon. Finally add the previously prepared walnut sauce and the remaining broth. Bring to a boil and cook over medium heat, stirring occasionally, until the chicken is tender and the sauce has reduced by a third. It will take about half an hour.

Put the egg yolks in a bowl and beat them with a whisk together with a ladle of the sauce, then add the mixture to the stew and cook for another 5 minutes. Finally add the vinegar, adjust the salt and pepper.

Pour into bowls and decorate with coarsely chopped walnuts and fresh coriander (or parsley).

Kharcho

- beef soup -

Kharcho soup (it is pronounced *harcho*) is very nutritious, consisting of beef, tomato broth and rice. The meat will turn out so tender that it will melt in the mouth.

Photo credit by *A. Savin* - WikiCommons

Ingredients:

* 1,5 lb beef
* 3,5 oz rice
* 2 onions
* 2 bay leaves
* 1 tbsp of coriander (or parsley)
* 2 teeth of garlic
* 1 tbsp of smoked paprika
* ⅘ cup broth
* 6 cups of water
* 5 tbsp of oil
* Salt

Chop an onion and put it in a deep frying pan together with the oil. Fry for 3-4 minutes, turning occasionally. Cut the beef into small pieces and add it to the onion, let it brown then cover the pan and lower the heat to a minimum, turn frequently.

After about 20 minutes add 1/2 cup of broth and after other 20 minutes add other 100ml. Cook for 20 minutes more, liquids will shrink. Add the rice, toast lightly then pour 6 cups of water and 2 bay leaves. Crush the garlic, cut it and put it in the pan with the paprika and salt.

Continue cooking over medium heat for 15 minutes. Then add the chopped cilantro (or parsley) and tomato paste, cook again for 5 minutes then remove the lid. Serve hot by sprinkling with chopped fresh coriander.

Megrelian Kharcho
- walnut and veal soup -

Meat and nut soup from the province of Megrelia can also be considered a stew, in any case it is a delicacy!
It is often accompanied to polenta with cheese.

Photo courtesy of *Megruli Sakhli Restaurant* - Tbilisi

Ingredients:

* 2,2 lb of lean veal
* 2 medium onions
* 1 cup of roasted walnuts
* 3-4 cloves of garlic
* 1-2 bay leaves,
* 1 tbsp of red chili
* 3 tbsp of oil
* Salt (quantity that depends on personal preferences)
* Spices: 1 tsp fenugreek, 1 tsp dried marigold and 1/2 tsp dried cilantro.

Cut the meat into small pieces and put it in a pot with bay leaves and 1 liter of water. Cover partially and cook for 1 hour over medium-low heat.

While the veal cooks, chop the onions fry them in a pan with 3 tbsp of oil for a few minutes, then add the meat that is cooking.

Separately ground the nuts and garlic several times. Add to the mixture the spices together with a little chili pepper. Stir thoroughly.

When the meat is cooked, remove 100 ml of water used to boil it and stirring gradually add it to the nut mixture. Continue to add and stir until the mixture has a soft and homogeneous consistency.

Finally add the nut mixture to the boiled beef. Stir and turn off the heat. Soup is ready!

Bozbashi

- stufato di polpette -

Bozbashi is a typical dish of Georgia but also of Azerbaijan and Armenia. In Georgia it is usually made of meatballs, but each region of Georgia has its own specific recipe. I propose the recipe of the Kakheti region in the eastern part of Georgia.

Photo credit by *Tkeawkin* - Pixabay

Ingredients:

* 2,2 lb lamb meat
* 3 onions
* Garlic
* 2 cloves
* 2 tbsp concentrate of tomato
* Aromatic herbs
* Cumin
* Pepper and salt to taste

Grind the meat and add chopped garlic, spices and herbs. Prepare the meatballs and then boil them for a few minutes, removing the foam produced from the meat. Meanwhile in a deep frying pan cut the onions and let them stew. (Other regions also add potatoes, peas, peppers. Vegetables should be cooked before adding water.) When the meatballs are cooked put in the pan with stewed onions, salt, pepper, spices to taste and toma- to sauce. Allow to cook, then when it reaches the desired density, serve hot with chopped parsley.

Ostri

- veal stew with tomato -

Ostri is a very popular spicy veal stew in Georgia, whether as a homemade meal or as a dish in restaurants.

Ingredients:

* 1,7 lb lean beef
* 3,5 oz butter
* 3 large onions
* 4 large tomatoes
* 1 tbsp tomato paste
* 2 cloves of garlic
* 1 tsp chili pepper
* 1 tsp dried coriander
* 1 tbsp oz of parsley
* 2 bay leaves
* 7 oz of marinated cucumber (optional)
* Salt
* Water

Cut the meat into small pieces and put it in a deep pot along with 2 bay leaves and 1 cup of water. Cover and cook at very low temperature for at least 2 hours, stirring occasionally.

When the meat is fully cooked it will turn out to be very tender. Remove the broth from the pot and store it separately.

Add the butter and salt to the cooked meat, then add the finely chopped onions, stirring thoroughly. Continue to cook over very low heat, onions should not change color.

Remove the skin from the tomatoes, chop them, pour them into the pot with the meat and mix thoroughly. Continue cooking. Add finely chopped garlic, 1 tsp dried cilantro, 1 tsp tomato paste and finally paprika and salt (if necessary). Add the broth of the meat we had removed.

Stir and continue to cook over very low heat for 5 minutes. Finally add the finely chopped fresh parsley and marinated cucumbers. Cook for another 5 minutes over medium heat and serve hot.

MEAT
AND FISH

Kutap
- trout with pomegranate sauce -

Georgia has thousands of rivers hundreds of lakes but fish has a marginal part in feeding. One of the few fish that are appreciated in cooking is trout. Fried trout with pomegranate sauce is part of tradition.

Photo by courtesy of *Tabla Saloon Restaurant* - Tbilisi

Ingredients:

* 4 trout
* ⅞ cup of corn flour
* 1 lemon
* 1 pomegranate
* 6 tbsp of butter or oil
* Fresh cilantro (or parsley)
* Salt

Clean the fish by opening it in half and removing the entrails. Season each fish with juice of half a lemon, butter and chopped cilantro.

On a bowl mix corn flour and salt with it breading each side of the fish.

In a large pan pour the oil and when it is boiling put the fish and fry at medium temperature for about 20/30 minutes, turning it carefully. The skin should turn out to be crispy.

Remove the seeds from the pomegranate and crush them with 1 tbsp to extract the juice. Add the remaining lemon juice, a little salt and a little chopped cilantro. Stir and leave for 30 minutes. Pour the pomegranate sauce over the fish and serve it hot.

Shkmeruli
- chicken with garlic and milk sauce -

Shkmeruli is a dish of the Racha region, named after Shkmeri a village located 1700 meters above sea level. Now you can find the dish in restaurants across the nation.

Photo by courtesy of *Tabla Saloon Restaurant* - Tbilisi

Ingredients:

* 1,7-2,2 lb whole chicken
* 1 tbsp garlic puree
* 1 cup of milk
* Salt
* Pepper

Open with a cut the chicken and remove the entrails. Sprinkle both sides with salt and pepper. Put it to cook in a well-oiled frying pan and adjust the temperature so that the skin quickly turns golden. Cover it with a lid slightly smaller than the diameter of the pan and put a weight (or heavy object) on top so that the chicken remains open and is crushed. After 6-7 minutes, check the skin to see if it is sufficiently golden and crisp. Turn the chicken upside down, press it with the lid and slightly lower the temperature.

While the chicken cooks, cut the garlic into small pieces and crush it to reduce it into puree.

When the chicken is cooked, cut it into pieces and put them on a baking sheet. Mix the juicy garlic puree with the remaining fat in the pan. If you want, you can also add some coriander. Slightly fry the mixture, taking care not to burn it. When it slightly changes color, pour a glass of milk, boil it for a couple of minutes and pour it over the chicken pieces. The dish is ready and can be heated in the oven.

Iakhni
- Braised beef with marigold -

Iakhni is a specialty of the Ajara region - people from other parts of Georgia may not know about this dish. Its intense orange color comes from dried calendula, which in antiquity was passed like saffron, since the latter was much more expensive. Then calendula has become one of the distinctive features of Georgian cuisine. A dish of the same name appears in various forms in South Asia and the Middle East. It is likely that this dish was brought to Georgia by the Ottomans.

Photo by courtesy of *Adjara Travel*

Usually at Ajara this dish is prepared with fatty beef breast. It is boiled until tender. Since from us it is not easy to find this part of beef we will use small ribs, which also have a fatty part.

Ingredients:

* 4 lb beef chops
* 4 cups of broth
* ½ cup finely chopped walnuts
* 4 cloves of chopped garlic
* 2 finely chopped yellow onions
* Sunflower oil

* 1 tbsp of salt
* 1 tbsp of marigold petals
  Dried "Georgian saffron"
* ½ tbsp khmeli suneli
* 1 tsp ground fenugreek
* Ground black pepper

Scald the small ribs in a heavy-bottomed pot with oil, turn them and brown them well on both sides.

Add the onions, salt, pepper, marigold and other spices. Stir well and cook another 5 minutes until the onions are soft.

Add garlic, ground nuts, broth or water until almost cover the meat.

Bring to a boil, then reduce the heat, cover and boil over very low heat for 2-3 hours. Turn the meat from time to time, until it is very tender and will easily fall off the bone.

Completely remove the meat from the bones, serve it with a ladle of sauce along with khachapuri, puri or corn bread.

Kababi

When we talk about kebabs in Georgia, as in the Transcaucasian regions and throughout the Middle East, we do not mean the *döner kebab*, which was imported from the Turkish chains in the west, but generically meat Roasted cooked on a spit. The Georgian version consists mainly of minced pork and spices.

Photo credit by *Lesya Dolyk* - WikiZero

Ingredients:

* 1,3 lb of pork a little fat
* 0,9 lb beef
* 2 eggs
* 7 oz onion
* 1 handful of dried berries (preferably dogwood or barberry)
* Salt
* Pepper
* Coriander or parsley

Make sure the meat is a little fat because otherwise the kebab will be too dry. Finely chop the meat with the machine. Cut the onion finely and put everything in a bowl together with the eggs, berries and spices. Stir for a long time. Let stand in the refrigerator for an hour.

Prepare a brazier or grill. Divide into small parts, and with wet hands give them an oblong shape to stick them on steel skewers or wooden sticks, press the meat well along the skewer.

Arrange them on the brazier and after browning, gently remove the kebab from the spit.

It can also be cooked without a skewer directly in a pan with a little oil, however, be careful to flour the oblong shape before putting it to cook.

Kababi should be served on a plate with lettuce and sliced onions. It can be wrapped in typical *lavashi* bread.

Mtsvadi
- veal skewers -

Mtsvadi is another type of kebab (*shish kebab*) where the meat is no longer minced but cut into large cubes. The Georgian version is usually in marinated pieces of veal, pork or lamb, cooked on large skewers and accompanied with fresh onion.

Photo courtesy of *Tabla Saloon Restaurant* - Tbilisi

Ingredients:

* 2,2 lb veal fillet
* Pomegranate juice
* Lemon juice
* 2 onions
* Coriander or parsley
* Paprika
* Salt and pepper

Prepare the pieces of meat beforehand removing excess fat and leaving them to marinate with lemon juice, pomegranate, paprika, salt and pepper for a few hours or better overnight. Thread the meat into iron or wooden skewers, season with salt and pepper. Prepare a brazier with hot coals, flameless, and cook them rotating constantly. When cooked transfer the pieces of the skewers to a plate and sprinkle them with sliced onion and cilantro or chopped parsley.

Mtsvadi
Chashushuli
- grilled meat with tomato and onions-

Grilled meat is very popular in Georgia, both as a family meal and on holidays and celebrations. Pork is the most popular meat, followed by chicken. In this recipe we show how to prepare a delicious family meal made from pork, tomatoes and onions.

Photo credit by Georgia About - Creative Commons

For marinade:

* 3,3 lb slightly fat pork
* 2 tbsp white wine vinegar
* 2 tbsp tomato puree
* 3-4 bay leaves
* 1 tbsp black peppercorns
* 1 onion
* Coarse salt

For the stuffing:

* 3 large and juicy tomatoes
* 2 large onions
* Dried hot pepper
* 1 tsp dried coriander
* ½ tsp dried blue fenugreek
* 4 tbsp oil and salt
(quantity according to taste)

In a bowl put the meat into small pieces then add a chopped onion, 2 tbsp of white wine vinegar, 2 tbsp of tomato puree, 3-4 bay leaves, 1 tbsp of black peppercorns and salt big. Stir, cover and marinate in the refrigerator overnight (or at least 4 hours).

Prepare the barbecue. Remove marinated pork from the refrigerator and strung individual pieces on skewers, sprinkle with coarse salt. Cook on the coals turning when necessary.

In a deep saucepan add 4 tbsp of oil with the remaining chopped onions.

Remove the pieces of pork from the skewers and add them to the pot.

Stir the ingredients. Cook them for 10 minutes at medium-high temperature, stirring often.

Cut the tomatoes and add them to the pot. Stir and continue to cook for 7-10 minutes at medium temperature.

Finally add the dried hot pepper (quantity according to taste), 1 tsp dried coriander, half a tsp of dried blue fenugreek and salt. Stir and remove from heat after 1 minute. Serve hot with cilantro or fresh parsley.

Kupati

- sausage -

Kupati is the Georgian sausage widespread throughout the country.
In ancient times it was obtained from the waste parts of the pig but today
we choose noble parts to obtain excellent spicy sausages.

Photo courtesy of Tabla Saloon Restaurant - Tbilisi

Ingredients:

* 8,8 lb of pork or beef (or a mixture of these two meats)
* 5-6 coarsely cut onions
* 7 oz hog jowl or fat bacon
* Sausages casings
* Mix of herbs to flavor
* 1 garlic
* Dried coriander
* Pomegranate juice,
* Salt and pepper

Pass meat, hog jowl and onions in the meat grinder twice. Add salt, pepper, garlic, coriander, flavors and pomegranate juice.

Gradually add a little broth to soften the meat, stir until you get a homogeneous mixture.

Soak the cleaned and washed casings in cold water and insert them into a funnel with a wide mouth, fill them with spicy meat (you can also use a pastry bag).

Tie them at the ends or close them with kitchen twine.

Soak the sausages in boiling water for 1 minute and remove them immediately. This way you can store them for a few days.

You can cook them in a pan or roast them. They should be served with onions and pomegranate grains.

SWEETS

Churchkhela

- sweet walnut and grape juice-

Churchkhela is the most curious dessert of Georgian tradition, it can be prepared with nuts, hazelnuts, almonds, pumpkin seeds or dried fruits of various kinds. We will do it with nuts but the process with other dried fruit is always the same.

SLURP!

Photo credit by Goosyphoto - Pixabay

Ingredients:

* 40 shelled walnuts
* 6 cups of grape juice
* 7 tbsp sugar
* ½ cup of flour

Crush nuts and preserve the entire kernels or half.

With a clean needle and a silk thread (or cotton) thread the kernels creating "necklaces" or better *churchkhelas* 18 -24 cm long. Make a knot at the end of the thread.

Prepare the syrup in this way: pour freshly squeezed grape juice into a saucepan and put it on low heat. During boiling remove the foam. Reduce the juice by boiling for about 3 hours.

Turn off and allow to cool a little, then add the sifted flour. Bring back to a boil, stirring with a wooden spoon, after about half an hour, the syrup will be ready. This mixture is called tatara.

Now you will need a stick (or another similar stand) to hang the *churchkhelas*. Look for a place to put it in suspension.

Soak the walnuts necklaces in the grape juice mixture and hang them on the stick. Allow to dry about 10 minutes then repeat the operation 5-10 times until all the nuts are covered with at least half a centimeter of tatara.

Leave to dry for 3-4 days until the *churchkhelas* is dry to the touch. After that wrap them in a napkin and allow to mature for 2-3 months in a dry place.

They will release a thin layer of sugar around.

Pelamushi
- grape juice pudding -

Pelamushi is the typical autumn dessert originally from Western Georgia. It is obtained from a cream based on grape juice. It can be made with black or white grapes. It is a simple but very good dessert.

Photo courtesy of Megruli Sakhli Restaurant - Tbilisi

Ingredients:

* 4 cups of *badagi* (concentrated grape juice) or 5,5 lb of fresh red grapes
* ⅔ cup flour
* ¼ cup thin corn flour
* 2 tbsp sugar

Remove the grapes from the bunches and wash them. Crush the grapes by spilling the juice, pass it so that there are no seeds and peels. Transfer the juice to a saucepan and boil it at medium heat.

Reduce heat and simmer for about 3 hours. The liquid should shrink to a little less than half. Remove the foam that will form over the juice during cooking.

Let the reduced juice rest over-night then strain it through a sieve.

Put in a bowl the flour, cornstarch, sugar and mix well. Add 500ml of reduced juice and mix with a wooden spoon, then with an immersion blender. Make sure the mixture is perfectly smooth.

Put the other 500ml of reduced juice in a deep pot and gradually add the mixture of juice and flour. Stir thoroughly. Bring quickly to a boil then lower the heat continuing to stir for 8-10 minutes until it thickens.

Remove the mixture from the heat and pour it immediately into molds, or in a bowl or simply into a serving dish.

Let cool for about 2 hours. The *pelamushi* should now be firmly solid.

Decorate with walnuts, or hazelnuts and the *pelamushi* is ready to be served.

Gozinaki

- crispy walnut-

Gonizaki is my favorite Georgian dessert because I love dried fruit. It consists mainly of dried fruits (usually nuts) and honey. It is usually served during the year-end holidays.

Ingredients:

* 20 oz walnuts
* ⅞ cup of honey
* 1 tsp sugar

Put the shelled walnuts in a frying pan already heated over medium heat and leave to toast for 2-3 minutes, being careful not to burn them. Chop walnuts and remove the skin as much as possible.

Put honey in a frying pan over very low heat, stir and lower the heat to avoid boiling. Pour the shredded nuts into the pan with hot honey. Continue to stir constantly with a wooden spoon. After about ten minutes, sprinkle with sugar and mix again. Spread the nuts over the entire surface of the pan.

Pour the boiling mass of *gozinaki* on a damp surface and level with the bottom of a wet spoon.

To avoid breaking the pieces, cut the cold *gozinaki* with a hot knife.

Baklava

- walnut millefeuille -

Baklava can be considered the most famous dessert in the whole Middle East. There are many nations that claim its origins. It is so ancient that his "invention" is attributed to the Assyrians, who alternated a dough of thin bread with layers of honey and chopped nuts, and then baked in the oven.

Ingredients:

* 1 lb crushed walnuts
* 7 oz melted butter
* 15-20 sheets of phyllo dough
 size of your text
* 7/8 cup of sugar
* 2 tbsp of honey
* 1 cups of water
* 1 tbsp lemon juice
* A pinch of cinnamon

Chop the mixer nuts with 2 table-spoons of sugar. Melt the butter in a saucepan. Put a sheet of phyllo dough in a greased baking sheet, lightly brush it with melted butter and repeat this action for all the other sheets. Stratify the sheets in the bowl alternating 2 or 3 sheets of dough with a layer of chopped walnuts.

Put the baklava in the fridge for 15 minutes and cut it into small pieces with a sharp knife.

Heat the oven to 180°C and bake the cake for about 15 minutes until golden brown.

During cooking prepare a syrup with sugar, honey and lemon water (you can also flavor with a little cinnamon). Pour over freshly take baklava out of the oven. Cut it again following the already imprinted tracks. Before serving, let it stand for a few hours or better all night. Decorate with chopped dried fruits. It can be stored in the refrigerator for 4-5 days.

BIBLIOGRAPHY

Merab Beradze, *Georgian Dishes*, Tbilisi 2011

Carla Capalbo, *Tasting Georgia*, Pallas Athene Publishers, 2017

Caroline Eden, *Black Sea: Dispatches and Recipes, Through Darkness and Light*, Quadrille Publishing 2019

Barbara Ghazarian, *Simply Armenian*, Mayreni Publishing 2004

Darra Goldstein, *Georgian Feast*,University of California Press, Berkeley, 1993

Olia Hercules, *Kaukasis: the cookbook*, Weldon Owen 2017

Olia Hercules, *Mamushka: Recipes from Ukraine and Eastern Europe*, Weldon Owen 2015

Kate Leahy, *Lavash*, Chronicle Books 2019

Tiko Tuskadze, *Supra: A Feast of Georgian Cooking*, Pavilion Books Ltd, 2017

SITOGRAPHY

foodfuntravel.com

www.saveur.com

planete-endurance.com

georgianjournal.ge

winesgeorgia.com

georgianrecipes.net

caucasus-trekking.com

tasteatlas.com

Made in United States
Troutdale, OR
11/18/2024

24968070R00066